Long Live King Dick

by

John Maher

Adare Press
White Gables
Ballymoney Hill
Banbridge
Telephone: (018206) 23782

Many thanks are due to Deborah McBride for editing this book.

ISBN – 1 899496 –'10 – 6

CONTENTS

The Class of '45

St Kevin's Primary School, Falls Road. John Maher is in the back row, last right

DRESSED TO KILL

My parents Tommy and Ellen lived with their brood of seven children, plus the three they had fostered, in a terrace house in the Whiterock area of West Belfast. It consisted of three bedrooms, a small living room, a scullery, a tiny bathroom and an outside loo. As you entered the living room, the cast iron fireplace was the focal point. It had an alcove each side of it. The left alcove nearest the front window contained our entertainment, namely a small radio. The right alcove was converted into a double cupboard. The top half had glass-fronted doors for displaying Mum's little bits of collectables, the bottom half had solid doors fitted. Both cupboards had fitted shelves. As Dad was unemployed (due to ill health), he had placed his favourite armchair in this corner and no one dared sit on it but him, his excuse being, as money was short he sensed good vibes when he sat in that corner and would soon get a brainwave to earn some.

One day Dad lit up his pipe, slowly puffing on it, staring at the garden through the front window, mumbling out loud, "That bloody garden, ye cudn't grow two carrots side by side in it, it's that small." He sat back in his chair and scratching his chin came up with an idea. "Nye that back garden is well fenced off an' it

5

has a shed in the corner. Aye, it's about twelve by six if me mathematics are right." He hit the arm of his chair with his right fist and yelled, "CHICKENS! CHICKENS!"

Mum rushed in from the scullery in a panic. "What's wrong Tommy? Are ye feelin' bad ?"

"Ellen, I've got a brainwave. We're going to keep chickens. Just think Ellen, I could breed them an' in time we could have eggs every day of the week. On top of that an auld roast bird wud grace the table every other month. Ehhh what do ye think of that girlie?"

Mum rolled her eyes to the heavens and shaking her head returned to the scullery, without uttering a word. She knew something would go wrong when Dad had a brainwave, it always did.

Dad remembered the rag and bone man exchanged young chicks for old rags as well as old jam jars. This would be how he could get the chickens without payment.

Listening to all this talk of chickens was Jimmy. He was one of the foster kids. Now, the rest of the family were quite ordinary and relatively sane but Jimmy stood out. His vile temper got him into more arguments with our neighbours than I care to mention. He never smiled, his lips were always puckered together and with a permanent frown on his brow, he looked a bad little git. In spite of this, one thing shone through, his love for animals. It was the first time in a long while I had seen a glint in Jimmy's eyes. I watched as Jimmy moved closer to Dad and gently tugging on his sleeve he asked, "Can I help?"

Dad put his arm around Jimmy, "Can you HELP! Com'n now, sure you're my number one man, you'll be in charge."

Jimmy's chest expanded with pride – he was to be number one man.

That's when 'operation chicken' began. In no time at all, three jam jars and a large pile of old clothes were placed on the living room floor. Dad retrieved Mum's coat, his own coat, plus two pairs of long johns, shirts and several pairs of socks. Calling Jimmy to one side, Dad informed him these items were needed when winter approached and should not be given to the rag man. The large pile was reduced to half its size.

It so happened that was the day the rag man made an appearance. We hadn't long to wait to hear his faithful cry of, "Yeany auld regs, jeem pets, bouttles." Translated, any old rags jam pots or bottles?

Now Jimmy's mind had been working overtime. He gathered several old newspapers, lightly scrunching them into a ball and proceeded to wrap old rags around them to make them look like twice the amount.

I was ordered to carry the jam jars while Jimmy took charge of the rest of 'operation chicken'.

"Nye John," said Jimmy, as he lifted the pile of rags, "follow me an' don't say a word, I'll do all th' talkin'."

He rushed out ahead of me, hardly able to see over an armful of rags, yelling at the top of his voice, "Hey Mister, how many chicks will ye give for these?"

"That's a fair bundle av regs yiv gat, an' three jeem pets as well!"

Jimmy gently laid the pile at the rear of the cart and took the jars from me and handed them to the rag man.

"Well young lad. I'll tell ye wut I'm goin' tay do. These chicks aren't too well. You take any eight ye want. If yer lucky ye might get two that'll live."

The chicks were put into a small shallow cardboard box.

Jimmy held the box close to his chest and shuffled up to the house. I didn't get a look in until we got inside. He had a spot already picked out at the corner of the hearth, far enough away so they would be nice and warm from the heat of the fire.

The family gathered around for a look at what seemed to be a box full of yellow balls of fluff. Jimmy kept telling us to move back and give them air. At that point we knew who the mother hen was going to be. Jimmy kept to his task of caring and managed to keep all the chicks alive. As the chicks began to look like chickens a larger box was found. Dad, much to his dismay, found himself pushed out of his corner to make room for the bigger box.

Now every Sunday after dinner all the kids went out to play in the street. Mum and Dad used this period to have forty winks. One Sunday, Dad awoke with a start to find a chicken on his lap pecking at his shirt buttons and the others strutting around the room as if they owned the place. That was the final straw. Jimmy was summoned. He knew by the look on Dad's face something was wrong. He didn't get a chance to speak before Dad erupted.

"Get those chickens an' that rooster out of here an' into that shed. They are nat to enter the house again – understood?"

Jimmy did his little bit of chicken talk. "Com'n chucky, chucky poo, com'n you as well Dick."

"Who in the name av blue blazes is Dick?" Dad asked.

Jimmy pointed to the biggest chicken. "That's Dick".

Dad replied with a little smile on his face. "Well, you named him well enough, for he's a rooster. Now get on with it. An' mind what I said – keep them outside."

Several months went by and we were into the throes of winter. One night in particular had been very cold. When we went to bed, Mum had to throw two or three overcoats (the blankets with pockets!) over us to keep us warm. Winter or summer, Mum and Dad got up early every morning to get things ready for us going to school, but in winter Dad rose first to light the fire and I always liked to be one of the first to rise as the bread man delivered fresh bread very early. Dad would wrap me up in an old shawl to keep warm. After lighting the fire, he would make me a cup of tea and a lovely fresh bap still warm from the oven. The butter would melt into the soft fresh bread. It was a treat I always looked forward to.

Dad settled into his favourite chair to have his breakfast when he heard a low clucking sound, "I think there's a cat near the chicken shed. I'd better have a wee geek." Dad came back into the living room, with a puzzled look on his face. "There wasn't anything there. I must have been hearin' things."

He sat down and reached for his mug of tea. He heard the same sound but this time it was quite clearly coming from the cupboard. Dad opened the cupboard door a few inches and closed it again very quickly. By the look on Dad's face, I thought he had seen a ghost. Resting his brow in the palms of his hands, he ordered me to get all of the kids from their beds at once and make them come down into the living room. It took a few minutes for all of us to assemble around Dad. We hadn't a clue what was going on.

Dad stood up and moved his chair out of the corner. "Who is responsible for this?," he guldered. Then he flung open the cupboard doors and with hands on hips, nodded towards the cupboard, his face bright red with temper.

For a split second all we could see were chickens dressed up in baby clothes, then all hell broke loose as the chickens tried to fly, jump and scramble out. Soon the room was filled with feathers and chicken shit. It took a while to get the chickens stripped of their clothes and put into the back garden We gave Dad a hand to get the room cleaned, then he lined us up.

"Right," he said, "who is to blame for this?"

It wouldn't have taken the brains of a gnat to find the answer. It could only have been Jimmy.

We all took one step back leaving Jimmy on his own while Dad stood shaking his head. "I should have known it wuz you Jimmy."

With tears streaming down his cheeks, Jimmy blurted out, "It wuz too cold for them sitting out there in that shed. I had to bring them in."

Dad took Jimmy into the scullery and opened the oven door. Looking Jimmy straight in the eyes he hissed, "The next time this happens they will all end up in there an' ye wouldn't need to worry about them feeling the cold. Nye do you understand?"

"I promise I won't do it again."

I can honestly say that was one promise Jimmy stuck to.

It wuz you, Jimmy!

LONG LIVE KING DICK

After the last encounter with Dad, Jimmy made sure the chickens kept to their domain - namely the back garden. On his return home from school, he would fill his pockets with porridge oats and sit for hours feeding and talking, or should I say clucking, with the chickens. He usually had Dick the rooster perched on his knee gently stroking its long neck telling it how much he loved his little chucky poos. Now 'little' was an understatement, it looked more like a bloody big vulture than a rooster, but Jimmy loved it and in return it loved Jimmy. Its affection for Jimmy didn't extend to any other member of the family. It paraded around the garden nudging its head back and forward. It had a strut like one of Hitler's stormtroopers. On occasions when any of us had to venture into its territory, Dick strutted around as if nothing was annoying it. But the bugger always managed to get between you and the back door, cutting off your line of retreat by stretching out its wings. The wing tips trailed the ground whilst its head darted to and fro. It made strange sounds as it went in for the peck. Ankles, knees, hands, face and even your backside were not safe from Dick's beak. There was only one person we would call or should I say scream for, none other but our Jimmy. When he came to our rescue, he always blamed us for giving Dick a hard time. To make matters worse, when that shit of a rooster heard Jimmy's voice, it staggered and almost limped over to him as if we had just given it a kicking.

The flaming thing would then cradle in Jimmy's arms for shelter and listen to Jimmy's soothing apologies. "Poor old Dick, what have they been doing to my chucky-chucky poo?"

After getting into the house safely, I confronted Dad. "You'll have to do something about that blasted rooster. I'm not going into that garden ever again."

"Ahhh get a grip on yerself son. It's only a harmless auld chicken," Dad replied.

Thank God Mum had been listening and stood up for me.

"Tommy."

"Yes Ellen?"

"A harmless auld chicken ye say! How long has it been since you were out in th' garden Tommy?"

"Well I've got no reason to be in it, have I Ellen?"

"You just totter on out there, that's if you think it's a fuss over nothing." Mum looked over at me with a slight grin on her face and gave me a little wink.

Dad went out to the garden.

Mum opened the kitchen window and whispered to Jimmy that his pal was at the front door.

Dad, now on his own in the middle of the garden, stared at us through the window, a smirk on his face, wide eyed and shrugging his shoulders at the same time, as if to say 'WHAT IS THE PROBLEM?' He soon found out.

Dick started pecking and Dad started screaming.

It wasn't too long before we heard an SOS message for Jimmy.

True to form the rescuer arrived as usual to console poor auld Dick.

Dad sprockled breathlessly in through the back door in utter panic.

Mum fought hard to keep from laughing. "Are ye alright Tommy?" she asked concerned.

"Alright? That thing is a bloody killer, it will have to go." Puffing and blowing, he continued, "It will have to go for sure, no question about it."

The rest of the day was taken up wondering how to get rid of Dick without hurting Jimmy's feelings.

"Ellen, I think I've got a good idea how to get rid of Dick," said Dad. "I'll tell Jimmy tomorrow, an' seein' as it's Saturday it would give him the weekend to get over th' shock. Just leave it to me."

The next morning after breakfast, Dad sat beside Jimmy with his arm wrapped around his shoulder and in a very sad voice began telling him, "Son I have very sad news for ye. In fact for all the family. Ye see son, we had to get the doctor out to the house last night. It was poor auld Dick. Before you ask any questions let me finish. Th' doctor had a good luk at him, an' discovered Dick was in severe pain an' that it wud get wurse. He said it wud be better an' less cruel to put Dick out of his misery. To save ye any hurt I'll put poor Dick to sleep so as he can go to chicken heaven."

With tears streaming down his face, Jimmy asked Dad to let HIM put Dick to sleep.

Dad was surprised and asked him if he knew how it was done.

"I think so," Jimmy answered in a subdued way.

"Well son, I'll go through it with ye so as ye know. First ye put Dick between yer legs an' hold him tight. Then get a firm grip of his neck, give it two good turns, then say good bye to Dick an' give one sharp tug. It won't feel a thing. Are ye sure ye got that son?"

Jimmy, head bowed, wiping away his tears, nodded as he shuffled out to the garden. He seemed to follow Dad's instructions. He got two turns of the neck okay, then let the neck go. He then proceeded to tell Dick how sorry he was and how much he loved him and started turning again. By this time Dick had twigged on to what was happening to him and trying to break free, forced Jimmy to the ground.

At the same Dad was shouting, "Give it a tug, give it a good tug."

Jimmy gave it another half hearted tug. Thinking he had finished the job, he let go of Dick and rushed through the house up to his bedroom.

Now I don't know if it was Dick's nerves or what, but it got to its feet and ran like blazes around the garden with its neck two and a half times longer than it should have been, its head trailing the ground.

Dad armed with a small axe went to put Dick out of his misery. With one 'fowl' swoop, its head was no longer part of its body.

I have never seen a chicken being plucked and made oven ready as fast in all my life.

In the meantime, Dad had found a box. He placed two large stones in it for weight, put Dick's feathers in the centre, his head at the top and feet at the bottom, while a piece of cloth covered the centre just exposing Dick's head and feet. It looked as if it was in the box complete. Dad dug a small hole in the garden then called Jimmy to attend the funeral. The lid was left off until he had said his farewell. The closed box was placed into Jimmy's arms, Dad gently rested his hand on his shoulder and they walked slowly to Dick's pretend grave. Dad let him bury the box then spoke some final words. "Here lies a well loved pet, a king among chickens. Amen."

We were at a safe distance doubled up with laughter. If Jimmy had caught us, he would have kicked the living daylights out of us all. The following day, Mum was serving up Sunday dinner. This golden roast bird graced our table ready for carving. My eldest brother leant across the table hitting the bird with the back of his fork and started talking to it, "Hey Dick, it's our turn to eat th' arse of you. Ye auld bugger."

At that point Jimmy came rushing in from the scullery. "What did ye say about Dick?"

Thank God, Dad was quick off the mark. "Calm down Jimmy, we were just goin' to offer up a toast." Holding up his cup of tea, he cried out in a loud voice, "LONG LIVE KING DICK."

After that another rooster was acquired and peace reigned once more in our house.

Long live King Duck

LET THE GAMES BEGIN

The Second World War had ended, bringing with it a yearning for normality from the elders who had to run to the hills for safety every time the threat of a bombing was heralded by a screech of siren. However, the air raid shelters, which had been erected in the streets for the people who couldn't for one reason or another make it to the foot of the mountain, remained intact for some years and the children used them to the utmost for their enjoyment. My mates and I decided to make some use of these grey-bricked monstrosities being somewhat short in the old toy department. Somewhere out of eyesight and earshot was a godsend to mischievous little imps hell-bent on doing anything that could annoy our parents without them knowing.

I was seven years of age when the war ended and I was ripe and ready for a bit of skulduggery and exploration of the outside world - the air raid shelters drew me like a bee to a honey pot.

Now, air raid shelters were not exactly advertisement material for the monthly edition of 'House and Home'; they were more suited to the farmers' edition of 'Byre and Piggery'. They were used as public toilets by drunks and kids, too excited to mundanely return home to have a pee in the middle of whatever game they were engaged in. They reeked of urine and had the atmosphere of a crypt. They were dark, littered with filth and comfortless. If your bum felt weary, the only place you could sit was on a long concrete slab attached to the walls.

We collected bits of lino and spread them over the dirty floor and along the concrete slabs to keep our feet and bums warm. Old boxes were used as tables and we pilfered whatever candles we could get our hands on to shed some light on the matter. Not being able to fill my mitts with the spondiblics to purchase the aforementioned, my mother's holy candles, which she kept for funerals, disappeared as quickly as they were blessed. The local priest must have thought the people in our area were dropping like nine pins every time she scuttled down the Whiterock Road to acquire another batch.

The shelter was very rarely empty of children telling stories by candlelight, mostly about the war and how we could have won it in one fell swoop. Cowboy yarns were also popular, but my favourites by far were the ghost stories. These did not begin until nightfall when the older boys infiltrated our domain. My mother would shoo me off to bed before dark and while her back was turned, I would tiptoe down the stairs and out the front door still in the same old shirt I had been sent to bed in. My short trousers and boots were tucked under my arm and as soon as I thought the coast was clear, I would bend down, arse mooning as I did so, and step into my threadbare trousers. My bare feet soon found themselves in lace-up boots and they hardly hit the ground as I raced the short distance to the shelter. They moved even faster as I made my way home after listening to a couple of ghost stories. After two or three ghoulish tales, I was scared witless. As I lay in bed shaking with fear, heart pounding, my eyes sitting out like ping-pong balls, my older brothers and sisters made things worse by threatening to tell my mother and father of my nightly activities.

But although those nights were scary, I felt sad when the council demolished the air raid shelters. There would be no more adventure stories, no more tales about the funny looking wee man with the moustache who we mimicked by goose-stepping up the shelter, our right arm outstretched and the index finger of our left hand stuck under our nose. But good comes out of bad, I no longer smelt like a public urinal at the end of the day, my nightmares decreased and new games began to fill my days. The street appeared wider and brighter, as if a fairy had waved her magic wand. Housewives stood at their doors chatting as the bread man and coal man sailed their way up the street without having to manoeuvre round the accursed shelters.

New games had to be invented. We made footballs out of scrunched up newspaper bound with string or elastic bands. The match started at two o'clock and ended in time for tea at five, that is if the ball stayed intact for that length of time. Each street had its own motley bunch of kids, (in fact that was the only thing we had in abundance, kids, kids and more kids. Our parents had to have their enjoyment too you know; money was scarce, their entertainment was primitive and the natives often felt restless!)

The atmosphere in our street was similar to Robin Hood and his Merry Men. The leader of the pack called the tune and we all danced to it. The girls juggled with small rubber balls or stones or skipped with ropes doubled up. Two girls held a rope in each hand going in opposite directions, thus making the skipper jump twice as fast while a rhyme was sung. If she tripped on the rope she was 'out'; in other words, one of the girls holding the rope took her place and she had the unenviable job of holding the rope. Boredom inevitably won though and the rope was tied to a lamppost. They swung round that until someone swung so hard, they would hit the back of their head and have to be carted off bleeding.

The boys made 'gliders' out of a plank of wood attached to makeshift axles at the front and back. Fitting it with old pram wheels, they steered it by attaching a piece of rope to the front axle. The most important person was the pusher or else the bloody thing stayed stationary. There was hardly a pram with a full set of wheels on it by the time the day ended. You were considered 'well off' if your mother had a pram with four matching wheels. Bicycles didn't escape the eyes of those in search of fun. These were divested of their spokes and with a bit of strong wire were shaped like a branding-iron with the letter 'U' at the end. You could push and guide the wheel for hours up and down the streets. Round and round it went, getting nowhere apart from ever decreasing circles. We tied a piece of string to the end of a stick and wrapped it round a pointed piece of wood and with a flick of the wrist we made it spin in circles until it spent its energy and stopped. This was known as 'whip and perie'. Other favourite pastimes were hopscotch, quoits and pitching, where an object was placed a distance away and we threw stones at it in turn to see who could get the nearest. The winner got the honour of placing the stone where he wished.

We were never bored or discontented.

These were for me, the summers of content. I am sure if God was looking down on us all then he would have said with a smile on his face, – YES I HAVE GOT IT RIGHT.

TELL US A STORY

It was the year nineteen and forty seven. Unemployment was rife, our area being no exception. As children, we tried in many ways to make a penny or two. Now if you were lucky enough to have a member of your family in work, you were almost certain to get a little pocket money each week. But in our house there were twelve mouths to feed and just enough cash coming in for my parents to manage. My mother had to supplement the income by making and selling things, such as iced and currant buns, haystacks made from coconut, treacle toffee and candy apples. She also baked her own potato bread and soda bread. Mum had about seven bottles of milk delivered each day She removed the cream from each bottle and placed it into a bowl. She then put the cream back into two clean empty milk bottles and covered each with a piece of grease proof paper. "Right John," she would say. "Be a good lad and shake those bottles till the cream starts to curdle. When that happens, you give me a shout and there will be a candy apple in it for ye." I started off at a very rapid pace, shaking as if I was possessed, you would have thought I was a member of a Latin American rumba band. It took a lot longer than I thought; after five minutes or so I would end off absolutely knackered. When I saw the milk curdle, I called my Mum to show her the finished product. She would lift the bottle for inspection and if she was satisfied, she would say, "Yes son ye have done a good job," and my chest would swell with pride and I felt like the king of the whole wide world.

"I'll start and make butter with this curd. Take a candy apple, son, and go on out to play."

I was hoping for a penny or two but I was only fooling myself, for my parents believed as long as you had a roof over your head, clothes on your back and enough food to fill you, any extra should be shared with those less fortunate than yourself.

Those less fortunate included an old tramp who called at our house every fortnight. Dad would bring him in and Mum would give the bearded smelly old man a slap-up meal and as he left Dad would put a couple of pennies into his pocket. I once asked Dad why he looked after the tramp and any other hapless beings that came to the door and gave them money and not us. He placed his hand on my shoulder. "It's like this son. Just think if God came to our door to test us and we turned him away, what would you feel like?"

"But Dad," I replied, "That's not God, he is the tramp that comes around every fortnight."

Dad raised his index finger gently tapping my nose with a glint in his eye, "You never know, you never know, that could be God you're turning away. Do you know what God looks like? He could be testing ye by turning up as a tramp, nye remember that."

I thought about it for a few seconds before I remembered that my mates were waiting for me at the corner of the street, never mind God calling at the door. I shouted at my mum, who was usually in the scullery. "I'm away out to play in the street, I'll leave the candy apple till tomorrow." I knew if I brought it with me I would have to share it - my father's wisdom had fallen on deaf ears!

When I got to the street corner, there were about six of my mates waiting for me. "Well," I asked rubbing my hands together, "What are we for doing tonight lads?"

They all answered at once. "We were wanting ye till tell us a story."

I had a very vivid imagination and I had learned how to put it to good use. Now out of the six, three were worse off than myself, the others, Plucker, Ballsie and Scratcher normally had a few coppers on them. I didn't want to appear too anxious so I rubbed my eyes and feigned tiredness. "Look here boys, I don't feel like telling stories tonight." Just at that Ballsie offered me a penny, Plucker said he would buy a candy apple and Scratcher made an offer of sweets. "Well seeing as you're forcing me, I can hardly refuse." I sent two of the lads to borrow a couple of candles from their mothers and the others to check out the three air raid shelters and pick one that hadn't been used as a toilet! As there was no lighting in the air raid shelter, we needed the candles to bring a bit of atmosphere to the story telling, I sat myself down on the concrete bench and the lads gathered around me in a semicircle. "Right lads," I asked, "What type of story do ye want to hear?" I was hoping they would go for a Western but they all wanted something different. I had to try and please them all, so I started off with cowboys and Indians at war and somehow German war planes were attacking the Indians and in turn space ships were attacking the German planes. I must have being doing something right as their eyeballs were sticking out like organ stops. Plucker was standing biting his bottom lip, one hand up the leg of his shorts continually stretching out his winkie and letting it go again,

Their eyeballs were sticking out like organ stops

Ballsie had his two hands down the front of his shorts and whatever he was doing, it was making his shoulders rise up and down and Scratcher had his right hand down the back of his shorts scratching his arse like mad. I kept the ghosts to the end of the story and by that time Scratcher had the arse nearly tore off himself with fright. As for the other three, God knows what state they were in for the last I saw of them was their backsides hare-tailing up the street towards home. It was now time for me to receive my fee. Ballsie gave me a penny, Scratcher put his left hand into his pocket, took out an old crumpled bag full of hard-boiled sweets using his right hand and retrieved a handful of sweets. He put the bag back into his pocket and offered me the sticky mess. My stomach churned at the thoughts of where the hand that gave me the sweets had been and I told Scratcher that I had a slight toothache and I would get the sweets off him at another time.

He answered, "Please yerself," and ambled off.

As for Plucker, I brought him over to my house where he paid my mum for the candy apple. I often wondered how they got those nicknames until the penny dropped. And thank heavens all young lads nowadays wear long trousers!

EIGHT TO YOU ONE TO ME

When I was running about as an eight-year-old just after the Second World War, most small time delivery men had to rely on the old faithful horse and cart. Our coal merchant was no exception. His horse was a Clydesdale. It needed to be a big horse to be able to pull a large cart laden with bags of coal. He was quite a large man and spoke very few words. It was very difficult to imagine what he would look like when cleaned up. He wore a peeked cap with a piece of canvas sewn on to the back rim. I think it was to stop the coal dust from going down the back of his shirt. He was a very frightening looking man, his clothes were covered in coal dust, his hands and face were as black as night and with white eyes and teeth, he looked like a bogey man. Most of the kids were scared of him. He always had a woodbine cigarette in his mouth and only spoke about ten words. They were "How many bags" then he gave the customer the price. He also had another word he used quite often. Every time he lifted a bag of coal off the cart he would say, "Fuck this for a game of marbles". He was very fond of children. Anytime there were kids in his way he would tell us to "Fuck off, ye little shower of bastards." Other than that his customers had no complaints about him.

It was his helper Dodger McCabe who seemed to cause the problems. Every ten weeks my parents would order eight bags of coal and two bags of slack, slack being small pieces of coal mixed with coal dust which were soaked with water and placed on top of the lighted coal. It prevented the coal from burning away too quickly. Dodger was in his late twenties, a tall gangly person with spiky hair and his clothes looked a size- and-a half too small for him. He always seemed to have a dewdrop on the end of his nose, which he kept wiping with his cuff, and he couldn't look you straight in the eye. There was no gate at the back of our house and that meant any coal deliveries had to be taken in through the front door, out through the living room into the kitchen then out to the coal shed. Well, Dodger was asked to throw eight bags of coal and two of slack into our coal shed so every full bag he carried through, he left the empty bag on the ground, so when he supplied the amount of coal that was requested he would ask some member of the family to check the number of empty bags on the ground then receive his money and was on his way.

I remember Dad saying to Mum, "Ye know Ellen? When the coal man throws in ten bags of coal it always seems more than the ten that Dodger throws in!" This was troubling Dad quite a bit. He was outside talking to a neighbour when he was let into the secret of Dodger's trick. Dad rushed into the house and couldn't wait to tell Mum.

"Ellen, what do you think of that blurt Dodger? Our next door neighbour was telling me that when Dodger is standing in for the coalman he takes several lumps of coal out of each bag and leaves it on the cart, then when somebody orders eight bags of coal or more Dodger puts an empty coal bag across his shoulders and the full bag he carries in hides the empty coal bag. Now listen to this. When you check the empty coal bags and you've ordered eight bags of coal he'll show you eight empty bags, but in fact, he only carried in seven. That's one bad pup Ellen. We have to be on our toes the next time he calls."

Sure enough, six weeks later Dodger called at our house. He opened the living room door and shouted. "The same again mister? Eight and two of slack?"

"Yes, that will do fine Dodger," Dad answered.

Dodger had the ten or should I say nine bags stacked at the corner of the cart,. Every time he carried a bag of coal into the house, my brother and I climbed onto the cart and filled the bags that were to be carried into our house to the brim as quick as we

Same again mister?

could with the loose coal that lay on the cart. When that was finished, my brother rushed into the house and out into the back garden while I ran around to the entry at the back of the house. As Dodger went back to the cart to get the last bag of coal my brother Charlie tossed the empty bag over the hedge to me. I rushed round and placed the empty bag onto the cart and I ran into the house as fast as I could for I didn't want to miss a thing. Mum and Dad, the brother and I were standing in the kitchen as Dodger threw his last bag of coal into the coal shed - or so he thought.

"Hello is there anybody there?" Dodger yelled out.

"What is it?" Dad answered.

"Ten bags you wanted! Ten bags you got! Just count the empty bags, pay me and I'll be on my way."

Dad started counting. "Ten bags ye say Dodger? I can only see nine, I think you must have made a mistake somewhere."

Dodger had a perplexed look on his face as he muttered, "I don't, I don't know, I don't really know how that could have happened mister. I'll throw ye in another bag." You could tell by the look on his face as he carried the tenth bag through that his brain was working overtime as to what had gone wrong. "That's it now mister, sorry about that," he mumbled.

"That's quite alright Dodger," Dad replied, "It could have been worse, I believe some coal man who delivers to this estate takes lumps of coal out of each bag and not only that, they say he carries an empty coal bag along with the full one and robs his customers out of a bag of coal. Well that's what all the neighbours are saying." Dad could hardly keep his face straight. After that escapade Dodger was on his best behaviour. When ten bags of coal were ordered by my mum or dad ten bags were delivered.

NUDGE, NUDGE, WINK, WINK, A FEW BOB IN YOUR POCKET

As well as the likeable characters around our area, there were others who would take advantage of anybody they could fiddle a few bob out of. One young lad, Eddie McKinley, certainly well and truly fitted the bill. My Dad was well known and liked around our estate, but due to his genuineness he was also known as a soft touch. Now Eddie was a very polite lad who always had time to stand and have a yarn with my Dad no matter what time, day or night and when Dad came into the house after a conversation with Eddie, he would always utter the same words. "That young Eddie is one fine lad. He'll grow up to be a credit to his parents", and Mum would reply every time with the same words.

"A fine lad! You can't see any farther than your nose. I wouldn't trust that young brat as far as I could throw him and that's not far."

All of our neighbours including Eddie knew my Dad kept chickens. I remember one winter's evening when Eddie called at our house and asked to speak to my father. Dad went out into the hall, leaving the living room door open. Eddie was quick to greet Dad, "Hello Mister Maher. How are ye?"

"Not too bad. What can I do for you?" Dad replied.

"Well, it's like this, Mister Maher. My cousin got some chickens given to him and he wants to sell them. I think you would get them very cheap. He was thinking of selling the chickens for two bob each and I remembered someone telling me that you kept chickens. And seeing as I know you, I'll get them for one and sixpence. Would you be interested, Mister Maher?"

"Yes Eddie, if they're fully grown hens and are healthy enough, I'll take them at that price."

"Give me a half an hour Mister Maher and I'll bring them round."

The half hour was no sooner up till the bold Eddie was hammering at our front door. "Are you there Mister Maher?" he shouted.

"Yes son, come on in," answered Dad.

Eddie pushed open the inner door into the living room, holding the chickens by their feet, one in each hand and one under each arm. "Would they suit you, Mister Maher?"

Dad had a good look at the chickens. "Oh yes, they're fine looking birds. If your cousin is selling any more at that price you just give me a shout." Dad put his hand on Eddie's back and guided him through the kitchen towards the back garden at the same time, telling my elder brother to slide the bolt and open the chicken shed door. As Eddie was making his way out to the back garden, my Mum was staring at him, her left eye half closed and her left eyebrow raised as if to say, "You are up to no good me laddo".

Eddie kept his head lowered, occasionally taking a sneaky look at Mum as he passed. The chickens were deposited in the henhouse. Eddie collected his six shillings and was out of the house like a flash. When my brother Charlie came into the house after bolting the hen house door, he tried to tell our Dad that the door of the hen house had not been bolted when he first went out, but Dad was that pleased at getting four good healthy well-fed chickens at a real good price. It was the next morning that things became a bit clearer. While Mum was hanging out the washing, Dad was on his way to let the chickens out into the back garden. He gently nudged Mum with his elbow and said, "What do you think of that, girlie? Four more chickens plus the twelve we have already means a lot more eggs."

Mum just shook her head slowly as if she knew something Dad didn't.

When Dad opened the door of the hen-house, counted the birds as they came out, he got to twelve and there was no sign of the other four. He stood scratching his head. "There's something wrong Ellen. I can still only count twelve chickens!"

Mum was quick to reply, "Is it any bloody wonder? How many times have I got to tell you about that no-good McKinley. He sold you four chickens, did you not listen to your son Charlie last night when he told you that the hen-house door hadn't been bolted. That little toe-rag took your own chickens from your own shed and had the gall to call around to our front door. And who bought them? It was muggins, yes, you. When will you ever learn? It's right what they say, "There's no fool like an old fool.""

Dad was speechless, Then, as if he was trying to put things right, he looked at my Mum and said, "That's it! There will be no more buying anything at the front door, do you all hear? That will teach you all a lesson."

From that day on Mum kept a close watch on Dad.

As for Eddie, he kept his distance from all our family.

THE ENTREPRENEURS

As young lads of the age of eleven or thereabouts, we were always in competition with each other, to try and make a little bit of cash, just enough to pay our way into the local picture house and a little bit left over to buy a few sweets and an ice cream. I was always on the look-out for anything that would pay a few pennies, from brushing a neighbour's path leading to her house to running errands. But there were two brothers in our area who were a few years older than us. I think Freddie was fourteen and the other, Hughie, fifteen. Now, they were head and shoulders above anyone else at the art of trying to make money. Both had a mop of thick unruly hair, which I was under the impression had never been combed since the day they were born. On top of that, they must have tried to give each other a haircut with a pair of garden shears as there were bits missing here and there, the results of ringworm or some other disease. If any one was looking for a stand-in double act for Laurel and Hardy, those two would have fitted the bill. In fact, Stan and Ollie were far too intelligent looking compared to Hughie and Freddie. Ollie, or should I say, Hughie, was the older and as he had one extra brain cell, he was usually in charge. The two of them scoured the local rubbish tip for about two weeks searching for old pieces of timber: any wood they found was tied into large bundles, and at the end of each day, they would carry these bundles back to their house and dump it all into their back garden. They then spent the next week chopping the wood into small sticks about six inches long and made them into small bundles, no more than eight sticks to a bundle. Hughie had picked up an orange box from a fruit and veg seller, nailed an axle to the bottom of it, and added two wobbly wheels from an old scrap pram to make it mobile. He then nailed two pieces of wood about two foot long onto the sides of the box, one piece on each side. That give him handles, either to push or pull the cart, The two lads loaded up their cart, stacked high with bundles of sticks. As all the households in those days burned coal, wood was needed to get the coal lit, that meant a lot of customers were out there waiting. They called at every house in our estate and within a few days were sold out. It was to be a performance repeated every other day. Gathering wood and chopping them into small bundles. One day, Freddie had a brainwave. With his earnings he bought an old rickety pram slightly bigger than the orange box. He explained to Hughie, that as the pram was bigger it would hold more sticks and thus make them more money. After a bit of deep thinking, he gave it his blessing. Now Hughie didn't want Freddie to have one over on him, so he decided to go for a bigger and better model. He had found a bashed up 'silver cross' type pram and managed to get it back to his house. After a bit of repair work, mainly, a half a dozen blows with a hammer plus a few screws, it was soon put right. Calling Freddie over he explained, that it was a far bigger pram; in fact, it would carry about four times as many sticks as the other one and, not only that, with its very large wheels it would go faster and they could get their stick round done quicker! They carried on their business this way for the next four months or so and low and behold, one day Hughie and Freddie appeared at the top of our street, Hughie, shouting at the top of his voice, 'Sticks fer sale.' With his shoulders pushed back and his big belly hanging over the top of his trousers, he had a smile on his face and a glint in his eye. Hughie was as proud as punch - the big time had come to them at last! They were on the first rung of the ladder. The 'Entrepreneurs' had bought a handcart. There was Freddie stuck in between the shafts of the cart that was piled sky high with bundles of sticks, with beads of sweat rolling down his face struggling to pull the cart along. Hughie would occasionally put his hand on the cart to give it a gentle push. Every now and then Freddie would let go of the cart shafts then spit into the palms of his hands and rub them together, then grab hold of the shafts, to give him a better grip. One of his customers had asked Hughie why he had bought the handcart.

"Well Missus, we thought our business needed to expand so I decided when we sold out of sticks, why not go into the removal trade."

Well let me tell you, some poor idiot trusted them. Their first removal job was to collect two wardrobes, a table, and two chairs from a house in the Falls Road area and take them to a house in the Whiterock area. The first half of the Whiterock Road is very steep and as usual Freddie was in between the shafts of the cart and Hughie was at the rear. They were really struggling to get to the top of the hill, and had just about got to the brow when Freddie decided to get a better grip of the cart to haul it over the last few yards. He let go and as quickly as he could spat on his hands, rubbed them together then made a grab for the shafts, except there was nothing there to grab. As the cart was heavier at the back and on the brow of a hill, it tipped backwards, Hughie went flat on his face, and the furniture which hadn't been tied down, fell off and smashed into pieces. The cart crashed and rolled about two hundred yards back down the hill. There was one sure thing. They hadn't to go very far to get scrap wood for their stick business; They had no energy to fight each other. Hughie, still lying on his belly, cursed Freddie in and out of hell. I would have loved to have heard them explain their way out of this mishap. It must have taught them a lesson, for it wasn't long after this incident when they traded in the handcart, got a donkey and cart and became rag and bone men. They must have thought things were going to improve greatly. Hughie contacted a wholesaler and bought a couple of dozen cups, saucers and plates, their intention being - one piece of delph would be handed over for every armful of rags. The two lads reckoned it would take about fifteen minutes to cover each street. They planned to work ahead of the donkey and when they wanted the donkey to come closer they could whistle and if they wanted to make the donkey stop, all they needed to say was 'wooah boy.' But Harry the donkey had definitely a mind of his own. Their first port of call was at the bottom of our street when they were halfway up, Freddie whistled for Harry. But no way was Harry going to move. Hughie shouted over to Freddie to leave it, that he would fetch Harry. Hughie sauntered down the street, grabbed a hold of Harry's bridle and tugged at it to get him to move. Hughie then fed and watered him and nearly beat the living daylights out of him, but he would have stood there until hell froze over. Harry wasn't for moving. Freddie came up with an idea. If they carried on working the rest of the estate and keep coming back to the cart every time they got an armful of rags, maybe Harry would start to move. Well they kept coming back and forwards until the whole estate was finished. As for Harry, he must have known it was time to go home for he started to move as the last handful of rags was placed on to the cart. I remember my sister Anne laughing very loudly as she entered our house. When Dad finally got her to quieten down, he asked her what was so funny.

Anne started to explain. "It was Hughie and Freddie and Harry the donkey, well", she said, trying to control her laughing, "I was standing at the top of the Whiterock Road just before you turn into Britons Parade when the two boyos and Harry the donkey reached the top of the hill. Harry started to stagger then stopped and started to sway to and fro and you'll never guess?"

Dad got a bit excited. "Come on Anne, hurry up, what happened?"

"I told you about Harry swaying. Well Harry let off a massive big fart and fell to the ground. Hughie and Freddie tried to get Harry to his feet but Harry couldn't get up."

Dad and I burst out laughing. Anne grabbed hold of my arm and shouted excitedly "I haven't finished. They took off all those leather things that holds the donkey on to the cart, then you wouldn't believe it, they brought the cart close to Harry and tipped the cart backwards. The shafts were sticking straight up in the air, then they put a big flat piece of wood between the cart and Harry. The wood was just resting on the cart and the other end was just under Harry's back. Do you know what they did next? Hughie asked a couple of men who were passing by to give them a helping hand and together, they managed to get Harry on to the cart and pulled the cart round to their house. While all this was going on, Harry was farting like a machine gun. When they reached their house, Freddie spread a bale of hay on to the footpath and then tipped Harry on to the hay and covered him with an old blanket and tied him to the lamppost. Then Hughie and Freddie went into the house."

Dad sat in his chair shaking his head and giggled. "There must only be two idiots in this world and they live in this estate."

We hadn't seen hair nor tail of the donkey for days until one day I and a few mates were standing at the street corner and Hughie and Freddie approached us. I called Hughie and asked him what had happened to Harry. I just had the words out of my mouth when Hughie replied with the slabbers flying, "Apart from the bugger refusing to move, when we brought him in through the house to get him into the back garden, the bastard went buck mad and kicked the shit out of us as well as the furniture. It took us an hour every night to nail and patch our table and sideboard. As for us, well Freddie let's show them!" At that point the two of them dropped their trousers exposing their bare arses which were covered in bruises. "That's why the bastard had to go, but don't worry lads, we're getting a horse to replace the donkey, and a new cart tomorrow afternoon."

Hughie interrupted Freddie at that point. "The horse we're buying is almost a thoroughbred and I think I pulled off a very good deal." There was no mention of carrying Harry home on the cart or about Harry sleeping on the footpath all night.

The following day I rushed home from school to see this fine specimen of horse flesh. My bladder was bursting and I flew into the yard to the lavatory first. As I stood having a pee I could hear a strange honking sound. My mum was looking out of the living room window and I could hear her burst into laughter. As I made my way back into the house I heard her say. "I have never seen anything like that before in my life."

"What is it mum?" I asked.

"It's Hughie and Freddie, they must have bought a horse and cart; that is, if you could call it a horse."

I was out through the door like a shot and the first thing I saw was a very large cart painted blue with its wheel spokes painted bright yellow. It also had a raised metal bench seat which held Hughie and Freddie. Freddie was holding the horse's reins in his hands, while Hughie had an old car horn squeezing the rubber ball at the end that made it honk. My eyes drifted towards the thoroughbred. My God, what a sight. It had a hollow in its back and its belly was about ten inches from the ground. You would have thought Two Ton Tessy O'Shea had been dropped on it from a great height. I walked around to the front of the horse and looked at it head on. What a sorry sight. Its ears were like a rabbits, they were just dangling down the side of its face. As for its eyes, I

If you could call it a horse

didn't know what was holding them in their sockets. All in all, I have never seen anything or anybody looking more sorrowful in my life. In fact this excuse for a horse should have been on the cart and Hughie and Freddie should have been pulling it along. I asked Freddie if the horse had a name. "Oh yes John," he replied, "we've decided to call him Flash."

I didn't know what to say, I was lost for words They continued travelling on down our street. There was no business carried out that day, they were just showing off their trusted steed to all who wanted to look. Again, Hughie and Freddie had got their brain cell working and decided with a large cart and this fine horse to pull it, they had to take their business further afield. Seeing as they had Flash, the world was their oyster.

It was several weeks later before I set eyes on the entrepreneurs again. In fact, it was a Saturday afternoon. I had just turned into the Whiterock Road from the Falls Road when I heard strange noises. As I looked to see where the sounds were coming from, I spotted Hughie and Freddie with a cart piled high with light scrap metal made up mainly of bed springs and old bed ends. Hughie had the horse's reigns in his hands while Freddie was beating the arse off poor old Flash. Every time he hit the horse he would cry out 'yo-yo', to make it go faster. Whatever they were doing it was certainly working. I never thought Flash could trot never mind run, but it was now running like the clappers. But the two boyos forgot one very important thing. Most of the Whiterock Road was laid in Tarmac except for about two hundred yards at the bottom of the road which runs onto the Falls Road which was laid in cobblestones. Any vehicle coming down the Whiterock Road has to start slowing down before reaching these cobblestones as the raised stones can be very slippery. Well, not Hughie and

Freddie! They waited until Flash had got its four legs onto the cobblestones, then Hughie pulled as hard as he could on the horse's reins, while Freddie's 'yo-yo' turned to 'woh-woh'. The horse tried its best to obey its masters but it hadn't a hope in hell of stopping. Its back legs met its front legs and the sparks flew from its hooves. As well as that, Flash's arse kept hitting the cobblestones. While this was happening to Flash, Hughie and Freddie sat on the pile of scrap totally rigid, their eyes sticking out like chapel hat pegs, mouths gaping wide open. In fact they were scared witless. Just as Flash was passing me, he looked me forlornly in the eye. If Flash had been gifted with a fifth leg, I'm sure he would have scratched his head and said,

"That's another fine mess you've got me into, you NUMBSKULLS."

'Lady Luck' must have been with them, for they continued to skid across the Falls Road without being hit by a trolley bus. After crossing over the Falls Road, the only thing that stopped them from continuing on down St James Road was the wheel of the cart hitting the kerb. The horse and cart over-turned tossing Hughie and Freddie into the garden of a large house. There was scrap metal strewn all over the road. As for poor old Flash, he just lay there as if to say, "Would some bugger put me out of my misery." It took about three quarters of an hour to get Flash back on his feet and the scrap metal loaded onto the cart. It was a miracle no one was hurt or any damage caused. I would have loved to think that these two boneheads would have learnt a lesson from this but somehow I doubt it. In fact, I seldom saw them after that, they must have opted to carry on their business outside the area. I hope though someone else had the pleasure of watching the antics of Hughie and Freddie

SPARE A PENNY OR TWO

There were a lot of characters around in the late nineteen forties and early fifties, but there was one in particular I must have passed by hundreds of times. He was known as "the man with no legs." This man was only ever seen on Sundays and always sat in the same place, at the bottom of the Whiterock Road, almost at the entrance to the city cemetery. He must have known this site was a prime spot, because not only did he catch the Catholics coming down the Whiterock Road on their way to mass in St John's Chapel on the Falls Road but he also caught the Protestants going to visit their loved ones graves in the city cemetery. The legless man knew that all those people would be a soft touch and he played to the crowd, for every stitch he was wearing needed to be thrown into the nearest bin, including his long dirty trench coat that he used to cover his stumps and his two empty trouser legs. His old worn cap was placed between his stumps and he always left a penny or two in his cap. I think it was to give everybody a guilt complex. Now as for his looks, he had a face no artist could paint. He never wore his false teeth and he usually had three day's growth on his chin. To make matters worse, he sat looking up at the people passing by him, with his mouth wide open and head slightly tilted to one side, never saying a word. He just kept nodding his head whenever a coin or two was thrown into his cap. He must have thought he had the look of a saint. To me, it looked like he had got his goolies caught in the cracks of the pavement. The legless man took up his position every Sunday morning around seven forty-five to catch people going to eight o'clock mass and packed up about twelve twenty. It was by pure chance I found out the time he left. One Sunday I went to twelve o'clock mass and decided to nip out early. On turning into the Whiterock Road from the Falls Road I couldn't believe my eyes because the legless man was putting two rolled up trouser legs into his pocket. Leaning over to his left side, he brought out his right leg and then leaned to his right and out popped a left leg. He started rubbing his legs very hard with his two hands, stood up and plopped the cap onto his head and hobbled on down the Falls Road. Being a young kid without much sense, I thought I had witnessed a miracle. I rushed home to tell my parents what I had seen. My excitement was short-lived after Dad told me that everybody knew the legless man had two legs. Then my Dad wanted to know how I got home from chapel so early. "I wasn't feeling well," I mumbled feeling very guilty, "so I thought I would come home early."

Dad called me over towards him and held me by my arm. "Well son, if you're not too well you'd better stay in for the rest of the day." Although his voice sounded menacing, in reality he was only trying to sound angry. He wouldn't have known how to be angry if he tried.

I fairly shit in the nest that day. That afternoon I was trying to get Dad to change his mind and let me go out to play. I cleared away the dinner dishes for Mum then went out to the coal shed and brought in a bucket of coal to bank up the fire. I was slowly getting Dad to change his mind when there was a knock at the front door. I was on my way to answer it when my Dad thrust a thru'penny bit into my hand and told me to give it to the man at the door. When I opened the door, I got the shock of my life because it was the man who sat at the bottom of the Whiterock Road. I decided to pull a fast one and keep the money my Dad was going to give him and I offered him a penny instead. The bugger refused to take it.

"A penny!" the auld lad said, "a penny you miserable little shit!" He was shouting at the top of his voice. "Ye'd see Jesus naked in the street, ye tight little bastard!"

I closed the hall door and came back into the living room, thinking I was going to tell my Dad something new, but he already knew. "It was the man with no legs but in the afternoon he becomes the thru'penny bit man and if he doesn't get a thru'penny bit do you know what will happen. He starts using a lot of bad language just as you have been hearing, so hand over the thru'penny bit and you are now grounded tomorrow night as well."

SECONDS OUT

I was baby-sitting my grandson one Saturday afternoon as he sat surrounded with games and hand held computer games, when I asked him did he ever get fed up with all that junk. He was very quick to reply, "Ohh noo grandad they're fantastic fun." Then he came back at me with a question. "Had you got a lot of toys and games when you were a wee boy?"

"Son," I said, "if any one of the kids in our street wanted to play cowboys and Indians, we would have to tie two pieces of stick together in the shape of a gun or use our index finger and pretend it was a gun, and if you wanted to be an Indian, we would have to find a long thin stick and some string and tie it to the stick in the shape of a bow and pretend it was shooting arrows every time you pulled at the string. As for street games, there were plenty of those to choose from and they kept us out of the house until bedtime in both summer and winter.

I'm going to tell you about an elderly lady called Morr McIlroy who lived in our street. She was a good bit older than your gran and a bit on the heavy side and she also had a big round face and her hair was bleached blonde." I was about to continue when my grandson rushed past me.

43

"I have to go now grandad, my mum's buying me a new video. You can tell me all about it when I come round again," and within a flash he was out of the house and away. I thought my grandson was the only one listening to my childhood stories, until my eldest son asked me, "What sort of a name is Morr?"

"I think it's short for mother, well, so I've been told. She loved getting all the kids in the street together every six weeks or so and would organise games for them to play. She would put us into small groups and allocate each group with a set of games. For example, the girls would play hopscotch and by securing a rope to a lamppost they were able to use it as a swing. As for the boys, she would have us playing quoits, blind-man's-bluff, hide and seek, running and long jumping. The winners of these events would be awarded with a candy apple or a handful of sweets. But there was one thing Morr McIlroy had a great love for and that was the noble art of boxing. That was one game I wasn't very keen on, the reason being I was a tall, skinny kid, in fact skin and bone would be more like it. As well as that, I had a large nose and I didn't like being punched, nor did I like punching anybody else. Morr always set out the size of the ring, usually the length of two houses and the width of the street. Most of the lads were around the same age, with the exception of one or two who were about three years older than the rest of us. Now I don't know if Morr had taken a liking to me or she hated the sight of me because I was always called on to have the first fight. My first opponent was Tommy Smith. He was about a head smaller than me but a lot heavier and as keen as mustard to get stuck into me. As soon as we donned our boxing gloves, Tommy was swinging lefts and rights. I'm sure if he had connected I would have been blowing my nose from the back of my head. That's when I started back pedalling. I headed half-way down our street, turned up Whiterock Crescent then around into Whiterock Drive and back to where we had started from, all in all, a quarter of a mile or thereabouts. Tommy and I were about a third of the way around the square but he was unable to land a punch on me and with me holding my right arm out straight, he kept running into my fist. Tommy was getting very angry so he made a mad charge at me and at that moment, I punched him in the mouth, loosening one of his teeth. That's when all hell broke out. He let out a loud scream and informed me as he gathered a handful of stones, "You hurt my mouth you skinny big nose bastard" and started to chase me, throwing stones at me as we ran. At the speed we were running it wasn't long until we arrived at the point where we had started from. Tommy threw his gloves onto the ground and went into his house crying his eyes out.

I thought that would be me finished. I had done my bit, but was I ever so wrong. Morr had another opponent waiting for me. His name was Josie and he was the younger of two brothers, about a year younger than myself. So off we went again taking the same route. Josie kept walking into my fist until his nose started bleeding. As we turned into Whiterock Crescent, just a stone's throw from where we had started, that's where Josie gave in. As he made his way back to the start all I could hear him say was, "Wait till my big brother gets a hold of ye, ye skinny, big nose fucker." As we got back to Morr, Josie's, older brother Ernie spotted the blood dripping from his brother's nose and he went berserk. "Let me at him," he shouted, "I'll kill him if I get my hands on him."

Morr grabbed a hold of him. I thought she was going to calm him down, but oh boy, was I wrong again. "Here Ernie, put these gloves on," she said. Ernie had them on and was almost on top of me. I had to go into top gear as I back pedalled. As Ernie was three years older, he was going to have to keep up with me. It wasn't until we reached half way when things went wrong. Ernie's nose started spurting blood. He stopped in his tracks and started going around in circles I thought for a minute he was taking a fit until I realised what he was looking for and found he had picked up a large piece of wood and started screaming as he chased me. "Stand still and I'll kill ye." He was snorting like a mad bull and I was off like a rocket, back to the safety of Morr. Ernie was in that bad of a temper, he didn't take any heed of Morr and continued to try and clobber me. It only stopped when Ernie's mother came out and slapped him around the head a few times and ran him into the house by the scruff of his neck. Morr must have taken pity on me for she took off my gloves and told me to take a good rest. I thought that was the games over for another six weeks but I was fooled again. There was still a big lad called Frah Burns. He was about three years older than me but he looked as if he was about seven years older. Now Frah and his elder brothers were into playing hurley and they were built like brick shit houses and that included Frah. The whole family were also well known for their bad temper. Frah approached Morr and asked her if the boxing was finished.

"Would you like to have a go at the boxing son?" she asked.

"I wouldn't mind but there's no one around," Frah answered.

"Of course there is." As Morr was answering Frah, she was fitting the boxing glove on me.

"What!" I yelled in utter panic. "That's Frah Burns. He's almost a man he'll murder me!" But it fell on deaf ears.

Morr had us facing up to each other and on the count of three, we were to start boxing. My game plan was the same as before, to back pedal, but this time faster than I had ever done before. Off we went taking the same route and we were already three quarters of the way round and the only thing that was punched was the air around us. Just as we were about to turn the corner into our street a few yards from Morr McIlroy, Frah tripped and fell forward. I tried to stop him from falling and it resulted in my thumb sticking into his eye. I was unable to stop him from falling and he hit his mouth on my knee slightly cutting his lip. As he rose to his feet, one eye half closed and bleeding from the lip, his

Come on and I'll kill you!

face went as red as a beetroot. With his hand covering his injured eye and his good eye sitting out like a marshmallow on a stick, he just stood there screaming. I was telling him it was an accident and I was very sorry but he just didn't want to know. He stared at me with his good eye and yelled at me. "Maher, I'll kill ye! I'll kill ye!" and then he ran off towards his house.

I felt I was going to need a change of underpants for it didn't take me to be a brain surgeon to know what was coming next and I ran into my house and closed the hall door. Whenever Frah lost his temper he always went to get hold of his hurley stick, his favourite weapon, and pity anyone who was at the receiving end of it. I hadn't long to wait. Frah was beating on the hall door with his hurley stick yelling and screaming at me to come out. While he was shouting at me, I was calling out to him through the open letter box how sorry I was but he wasn't listening. I was only saved from the rantings of Frah by my next door neighbour as he threatened to stick the poker he was holding up Frah's arse if he didn't clear off. As Frah walked away from my house, he was shaking his hurley stick at me as I was peering out through the letter box. "I'll get you tomorrow, Maher, just you wait and see." Thank God it was the summer holidays and I was able to keep out of his way for a few days until he was able to calm down and things returned to normal. As for Morr McRory's games, I was determined to develop a sore hand every time the boxing was arranged and I kept this up until I was too old to take part in the children's street games anymore.

THRIFTINESS

A s I watch people today discarding items they no longer need or want, it sticks in my craw. This feeling probably stems back to when I was a young kid and has been with me to the present day, much to the embarrassment of my family. I remember one Sunday I had taken the family out for a drive in the car and we stopped to buy some sweets. Just as we were ready to drive off, I spotted a skip at the side of the shop which was filled to overflowing, and sitting on top of the rubbish were several boxes of jam jars. I was thinking out loud and said, "There's a fortune sitting on top of that rubbish." Our youngest girl tugged at the back of my collar asking. "What did you say daddy?"

My dear lady wife answered the child. "Don't pay any attention to your da. He's off on one of his trips."

How right she was, because seeing the jam jars brought me back to nineteen and forty six when a penny and a few jam jars would have secured your entertainment for the day. There were three picture houses on the Falls Road then, The 'Broadway,' the 'Clonard' and the 'Diamond'. There was also the 'Arcadian' in Albert Street and the ' Central' in Smithfield. As the 'Broadway,' and the 'Clonard' looked too posh we usually kept to the other three for they all accepted jam jars as an entrance fee. A crowd of us used to go to the 'Diamond' on a Saturday morning to see a Hop-a-Long Cassidy or a Roy Rogers film. Everybody bought either a candy apple or a penny worth of sweets from the little shop nearby. The picture house had a concrete floor which slanted towards the screen and there was a gully tracked into the floor just below the film screen which always smelled of disinfectant. We would sit eyes glued to the screen and then the silence would be broken by the sound of hissing, or should I say pissing, and the noise of rushing water. At that point everybody would lift their feet till the weather had dried up!. Then you were tortured by the kids at the back of the hall who decided they no longer wanted their half-eaten candy apples and started throwing them at the kids a couple of rows in front. Sometimes, you would only be in the picture hall for around half an hour when the carry on would get so bad, the film would stop, the lights switched on and the attendants would slap the head of everyone until the hall was cleared.

Another favourite haunt which accepted jam jars was the Arcadian. It was a more respectable picture house than the Diamond. Every weekend the Arcadian would run a talent contest but for every good act that passed through, there were twenty bad ones and that's were the fun came in. A number of the audience carried with them bags of rotten apples, tomatoes and pears. I can recall seeing an old bloke starting to sing, but he only got as far as the first line when the audience started to heckle him, asking him to start singing through his mouth and not through his backside. The old guy stopped singing and hurled verbal abuse back at the audience. That was the biggest mistake he could ever have made, for I have never seen as much fruit fly through the air in all my life and at least ninety per cent found its target. The mixture that was thrown was so squelchy it was dripping off him but he managed to get down off the stage and tried to attack the audience. It took quite a while to remove him and get the stage cleaned up to enable the rest of the acts to continue. There was one other picture house which I only visited on one occasion.

That was the 'Central' which was in the Smithfield area. It was a very small and grubby little picture house and was flea infested. There was only one thing I or anybody else would say which was, if you entered that picture house at eight, you would come out half ate.

Things have certainly changed now days!

I caught sight of my naked body in the bathroom mirror as I removed my partial denture while preparing for bed the other night.

"Is that me?" I asked. "Is that old geezer with the paunch surrounded by those luxurious tiles really *wee* John Maher, the wee lad from the Whitewell Road?'

"OK! So you still think of yourself as a young fellow and now you're getting to be past your sell-by-date."

"Now's the time to count your blessings. Your parents were poor in cash but rich with love. Compared to them, you have a great lifestyle with enough love and laughter to warm you through your old age, although your bones creak and the rest of your bits appear to be falling off, not functioning, drying up or leaking."

I imagine I will always be able to feel grateful and look back with affection.